Mystie's Activities for

Bereaved

Middle School

Students

Utilizing
For the Love of Mr. Max

I0140892

KIDS' GRIEF RELIEF

Hi, I'm Mystie.
What's
Dragon - You - Down ?

www.KidsGriefRelief.org
A 501(c)(3) NonProfit
Grief Support to Empower Bereaved Children

MY FAMILY MEMBERS

Circle the ones you live with

My special person who died: _____

What goes on in my Grief Support Group, stays in my Grief Support Group.

signed_____

date_____

Who is in my Grief Support Group?

Activity 2

What Grief is like for me:

Draw a picture to represent how you feel.

THERE IS NO "RIGHT WAY" TO GRIEVE.

YOU ARE GRIEVING THE WAY YOU NEED TO.

Other People who are grieving over the death of my loved one:

_____

_____

_____

_____

People who are supporting me:

_____

_____

_____

_____

_____

Activity 5

What can you say to someone who has lost a loved one?

You can speak
WORDS OF COMPASSION

"I feel sad to hear about the death of your _____. I'm here if you need someone to talk to."

"I'm sorry to hear about the death of _____. You must miss him very much."

"I know you feel really sad about _____ dying. It's okay to feel sad and upset about it."

"I'm sorry to hear abou the death of your _____. I guess this is a hard time for you."

"Your _____ loved you a lot. I know you're going to miss her. I'll bet you have lots of great memories about her.

You've had many experiences throughout your life. Which ones do you always want to remember?

Write down at least five different memories that mean something to you.

This timeline ends with the death of your loved one. You will have an opportunity to add to your timeline in another lesson.

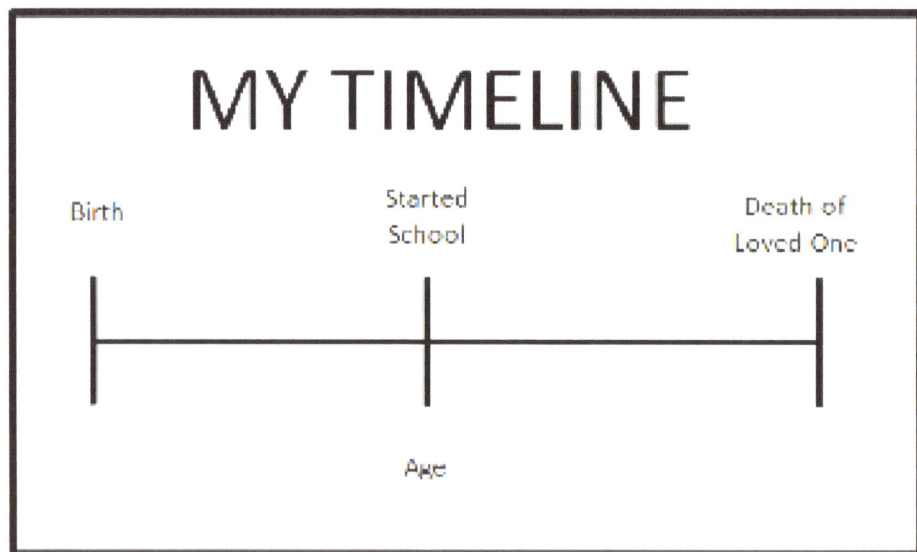

MY TIMELINE

Birth

Started
School

Death of
Loved One

Age

As you listen to others share their timeline, notice how different some of your memories are from the other students in your group.

Also notice that some are the same as others.

It's important to tell your story about the death of your loved one.

What happened is part of your life forever.

It's unique.

WRITE YOUR STORY ON THE NEXT PAGE USING THE PROMPTS BELOW

- Tell something about the relationship you had with your loved one before he/she died.

- What was your relationship like just before he/she died?"

- Tell about the day your loved one died. Where were you? How did you find out? Who was with you? Where did you go? How did you feel?

- Tell about the memorial service for your loved one. Was there a funeral? Did you participate? Was your loved one cremated? If so, where are the ashes?

- How did the rest of your family and friends react to the death?

- What was the worst part of the experience?

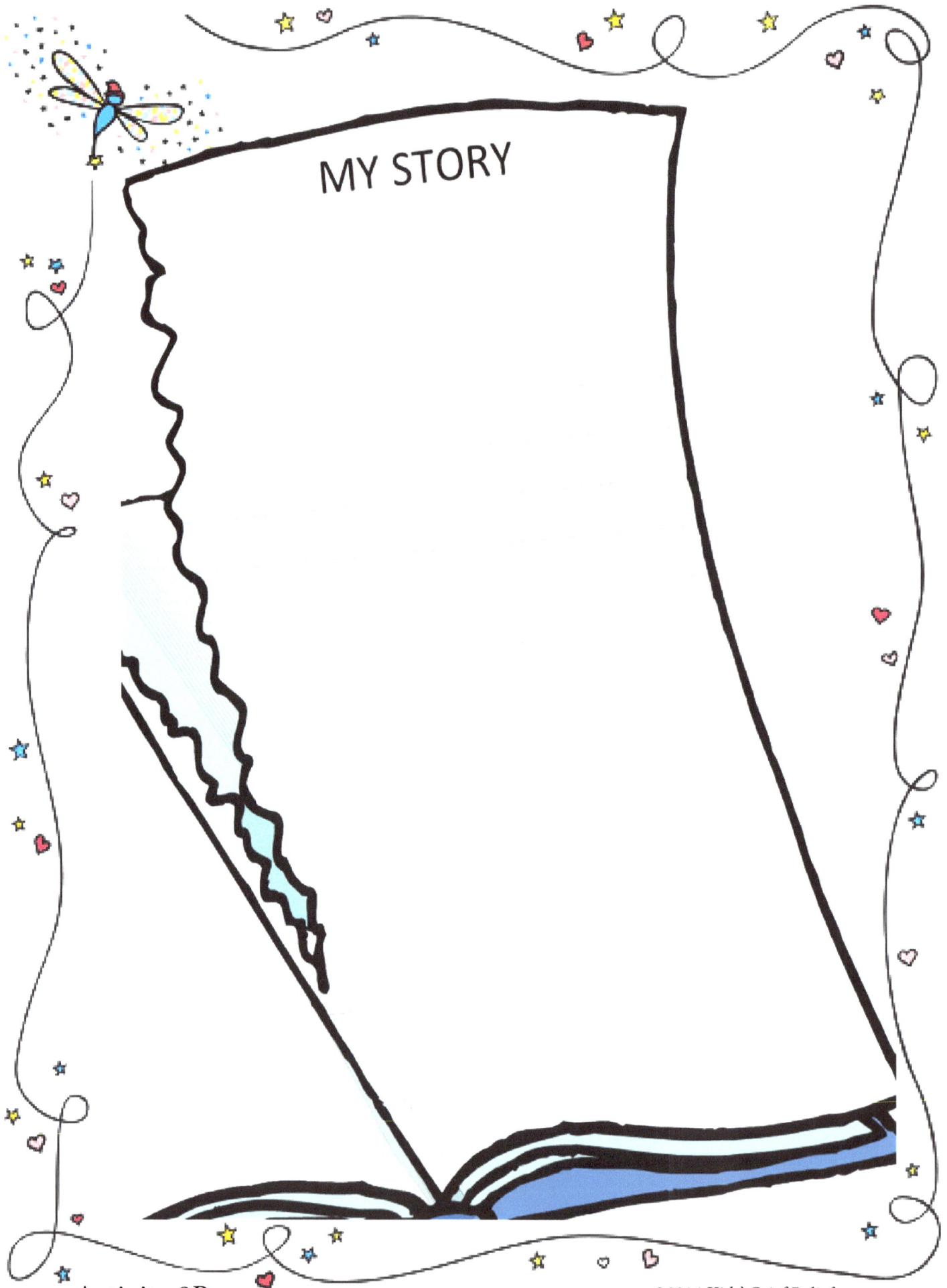

MY STORY

Do other people in your life know how you are really feeling?

Does the outside you (what people see) match how you feel inside?

Sometimes when we grieve, we feel like we're wearing a mask. That's okay.

OUTSIDE ME   INSIDE ME

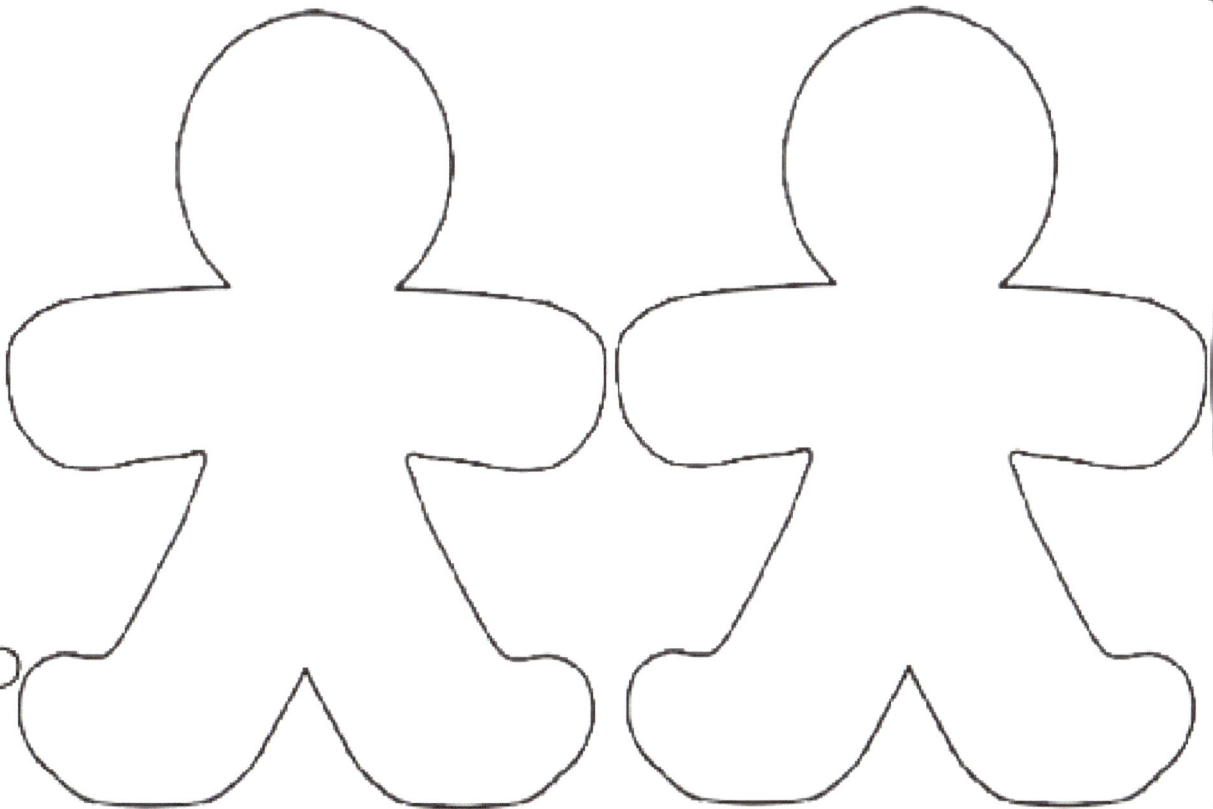

Activity 10

Validation is a specific way to practice Compassion. When you validate someone, you warmly say back to them exactly what he/she said. It feels good to be validated.

I'm afraid someone else I love might die.

You said you're afraid someone else you love might die. I get that.

Complete this sentence:

The hardest thing for me right now is

_____.

Read your sentence aloud.
Choose another group member to validate you.

Activity 11

1 What is the first and last name of your special person ?	**2** Did your special person teach you anything ?	**3** Do you know your special person's birthday ? (Day/Month/Year)	**4** Was your special person buried or cremated ?	**5** Did your special person like to wear jewelry ? What kind ?
6 Describe a special holiday spent with your special person.	**7** Tell about the last time you saw your special person.	**8** What name did your special person call you ?	**9** Tell about a funny moment with your special person.	**10** Describe a trip you took with your special person.
11 Tell about what kind of clothes your special person liked to wear.	**12** Tell about an object that reminds you of your special person.	**13** What kind of music did your special person enjoy ?	**14** What kind of movies did your special person like to watch ?	**15** Did your special person ever have a pet ?
16 Did your special person have a favorite saying - what was it ?	**17** Tell about a sad memory with your favorite person.	**18** Tell about some of the people who loved your special person.	**19** What one thing always makes you think about your special person ?	**20** What's your favorite photo of your special person ? Describe it.
21 Tell about something your special person loved to do.	**22** What time of day do you feel "dragged-down" over the death of your special person ?	**23** What's the one thing you will miss MOST about your special person ?	**24** Do you feel peaceful about the way your special person was buried ? Why ?	**25** Tell about a gift you gave your special person.

Activity 13

What special things do you have to remind yourself about your special someone who died? Make a list.

1

2

3

4

5

6

Where do you keep your special things?

You're probably thinking a lot
about your loved one.

Fill in the blanks below
with some of your thoughts.

I wonder _____.

I try _____.

I understand _____.

I want _____.

I learned _____.

I wish _____.

I am _____.

Where do you believe your
special person's spirit is?

Share your vision
with the other students in your group,
remembering that everyone has their
own ideas about the afterlife.

Here's another opportunity to
validate each other.

Listen to each other's plans for the next year,
then choose one experience to validate.

Add something positive
after you validate your friend.

You can say something like,
"that sounds like fun" or "good for you".

Next summer I'm going
to be a junior counselor
at my camp.

Wow ! Next summer you're
going to be a junior
counselor at your camp.
I'll bet you're going to have
lots of fun.

Wisdom from a Mystical Dragonfly

Emotions are an important part of life.
You experience positive and negative
emotions all the time.

Look at the faces below.
Can you name some emotions
by looking at the faces?

The word "emotion" can be defined as
"energy in motion."

You experience different emotions
in different situations.

When you're grieving, your emotions, or *energies-in-motion* may make you feel as if you were on a roller coaster! Some days you feel okay, some days you may feel very upset. Some days you might feel angry and confused. Some days you might feel that your life is upside down!

It's normal to feel as if you are on a roller coaster when you're grieving.

Eventually, your "ride" will even out.

As you feel and express your different emotions in healthy ways, you will feel better.

Activity 18B

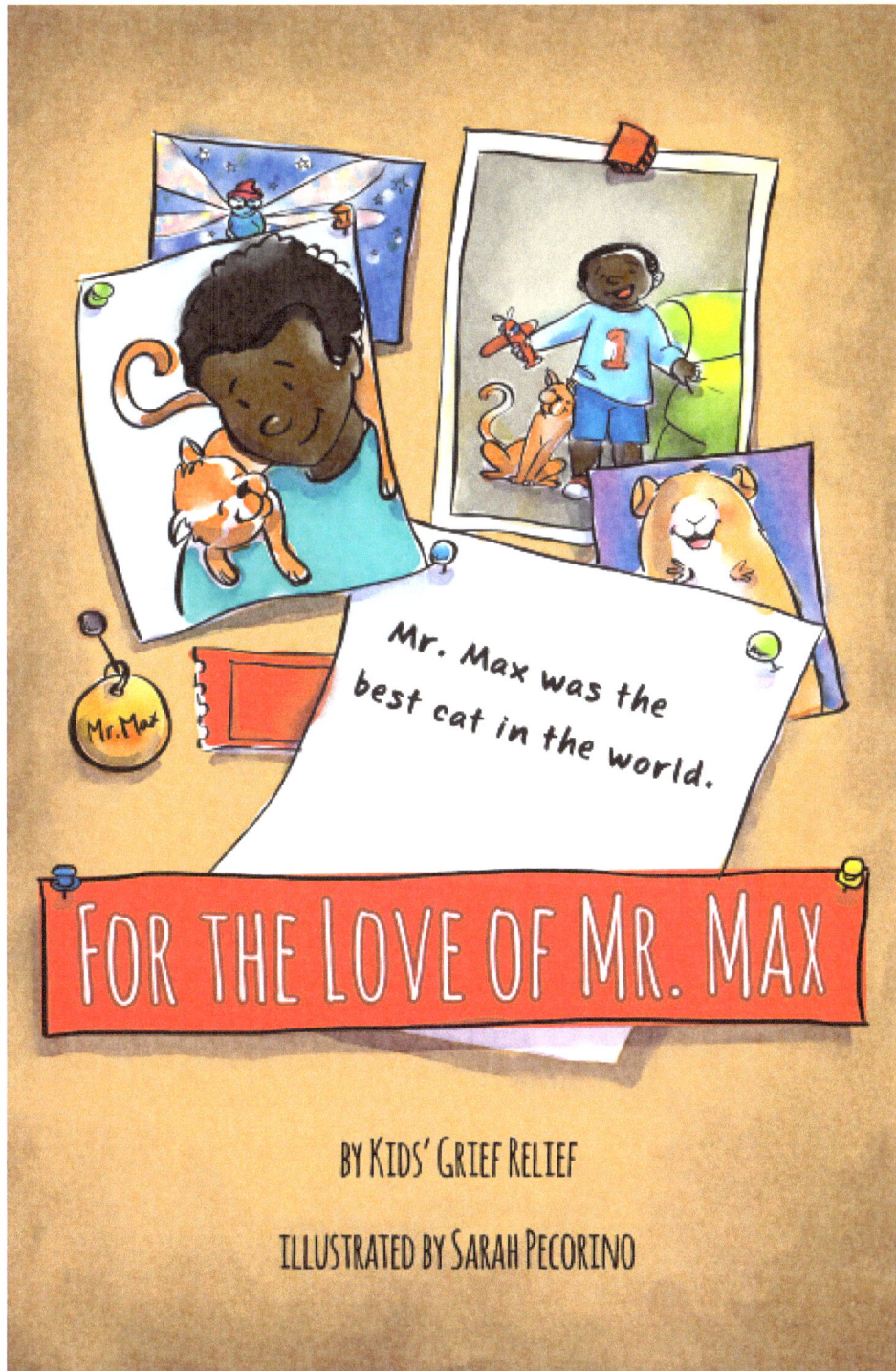

Mr. Max was the best cat in the world.

FOR THE LOVE OF MR. MAX

BY KIDS' GRIEF RELIEF

ILLUSTRATED BY SARAH PECORINO

For the Love of Mr. Max

1. MAX

2. GINGER

3. NO WAY!

4. ANGER

Activity 19

For the Love of Mr. Max

(continued)

5. ANGER IS AS ANGER DOES

6. BIG TROUBLE

7. MYSTIE

8. PICTURE THIS

Activity 19

What can I do
when I feel a stuck emotion?

I can...

1.

2.

3.

4. Still myself and take a few deep breaths.

WHAT YOU THINK MATTERS

Guess how many thoughts most people
think in one day? Some say 50,000 !

Positive thoughts create positive experiences.

Yet, when you're grieving, you probably have a
lot of dragged-down thoughts. That's normal.

Any of these feel familiar?

It's terrible that I'll never see _____ again.

I wish I could change what happened.

My life is all messed up now.

I keep thinking about how _____ died.

If only I could have _____ maybe _____ wouldn't have died.

It's not fair!

What if someone else dies?

I should have been nicer to _____.

Activity 22

Now that you've thrown away your "trash thoughts", it's time to replace them with powerful, affirming thoughts.

An affirming thought declares a truth.

Your true nature is Love. Love is more than an emotion because it's energy is always present inside you. Love IS you!

The love you feel for your loved one is forever. The energies of grief will move through you, but Love remains. That's Powerful!

Affirming thoughts come from Love, which means they come from the truth of who you are.

Take a look at the thoughts on the next page.

Can you feel the POWER in those thoughts?

1. I am brave.

2. I am smart enough to understand what happened.

3. It feels good to talk to others about what happened.

4. I have my own unique feelings about death.

5. I have special memories of _____ that I will always treasure.

6. I like who I am.

7. I am grateful for all the people who love me.

8. I am a powerful kid!

9. I can find healthy ways to let go of anger.

10. I am capable to handle what's going on in my life.

11. I choose relationships with people who appreciate me for who I am.

Activity 23B

Activity 24

Dear _____

_____

_____

_____

_____

_____

_____

_____

_____

_____

Love Always,

_____

Activity 26A

Dear _____

_____

_____

_____

_____

_____

_____

_____

_____

_____

_____

_____

_____

Love Always,

_____

Activity 26B

FOREVER CALENDAR

During each and every day,
We Love them.

During each and every night,
We Love them.

During each and every week,
We Love them.

During each and every month,
We Love them.

During each and every season,
We Love them.

During each and every year,
We Love them.

As the days turn into weeks, turn into months,
turn into seasons, turn into years,
We Love them;
Forever.

Activity 28

Hi Kids!

If you'd like to know more about me and my mystical, magical ways, email me at mystie@kidsgriefrelief.org

I'll send you MY story about how I moved through grief.

It all started when I made the decision to come to Earth. Did you know I'm from another planet?

WARNING—it's SAD yet really POWERFUL!

You'll learn about my best friend Darvy, the earth dragonfly!

Hope we can continue to be friends!

www.ingramcontent.com/pod-product-compliance
Lightning Source LLC
LaVergne TN
LVHW072110070426
835509LV00002B/101